The Little Book of Apologies

Is it so hard to say sorry?

Written by Karen Martin
Illustrations by Thomas Corboy

Copyright © 2025 KazJoyPress

The Moral Rights of the illustrator **Thomas Corboy**
have been asserted.

All rights reserved. No part of this book may be reproduced
or used in any manner without written permission except for
the use of quotations for a book review.

For more information email kazjoypress@gmail.com

First published in Australia in June 2025 by
KazJoyPress (Australia) **www.kazjoypress.com**

Book formatting & co-design by Working Type Studio

SEL031000 SELF-HELP / Personal Growth / General
ISBN: 978-1-7636685-3-9 (Paperback)
ISBN: 978-1-7636685-2-2 (Hardcover)

A catalogue record for this
book is available from the
National Library of Australia

Dedicated to all the exes out there who couldn't or wouldn't say sorry

noun: apology

1. a way of saying you're sorry
2. an acknowledgement of feeling bad
3. a wish that you hadn't done what you did

Relationships are great – until they're not. One minute, you're in a bubble of bliss; the next, you're smack in the middle of an argument that seemed to come from nowhere. When that happens, a good apology can help patch things up. But what happens when the apology given just doesn't *feel* right?

A real apology is heartfelt. It shows care and concern and involves admitting a screw up. It means taking responsibility for whatever was said or done that triggered the mess in the first place.

Saying sorry isn't just a quick fix or a throwaway line. A real apology can have a silver lining that leads to:

- establishing boundaries about what's okay and what's not in the relationship
- showing genuine regret for what happened
- learning from mistakes and finding better ways to handle tough situations
- creating space for meaningful conversation, and
- if you are in an intimate relationship (sometimes) make-up sex.

It may not resolve everything, but a sincere *I'm sorry* can lighten the load, ease the guilt and rebuild trust.

To truly say sorry can be difficult for some people. It may reveal too much – their pride, shame, guilt. For others, it can feel like admitting weakness or vulnerability – that they were actually wrong. And there are some who fear the fallout of taking responsibility.

Sometimes, resistance to apologise is attached to past trauma or childhood wounds, where expressing remorse feels impossible. Or a self-protective habit of refusing to apologise is too strongly entrenched.

But here's the problem: not apologising is a false emotional economy. Sure, it protects a fragile ego in the short term, but it also fuels tension, enflames unresolved conflicts, and erodes trust.

What can be worse is the *sorry not sorry* - the non-apology. This is disguised to sound like an apology but if you listen carefully, you may find it shifts blame to avoid accountability. It is a peace offering wrapped in a giant '*not my fault*' ribbon. Our empathy in these situations can leave us in a tangled mess of confusion and doubt.

That's where *The Little Book of Apologies* comes in. It's a curated collection of *I'm sorry* statements for all sorts of situations. Think of it as a guide to identify what's on offer – a heartfelt apology, a half-hearted one, or something in between. It's up to you whether you want to accept it. Or not.

Good luck navigating this rocky boat.

love Karen xx

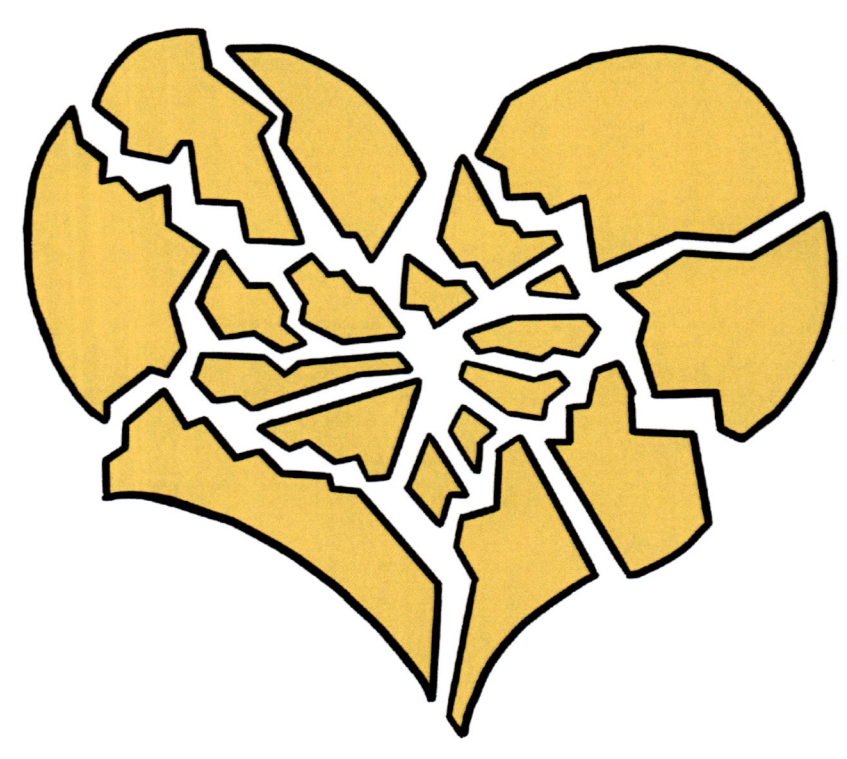

Being a weird mum
builds character.

I just got upset
in the heat
of the moment.
You know
I didn't mean it.

I'm sorry **but** if you had listened the first time.

I was joking. Can't you take a joke?

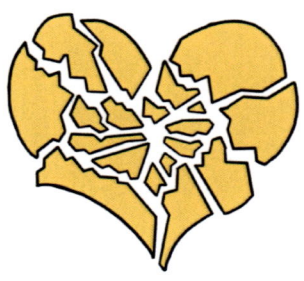

I'm sorry.

Happy now?

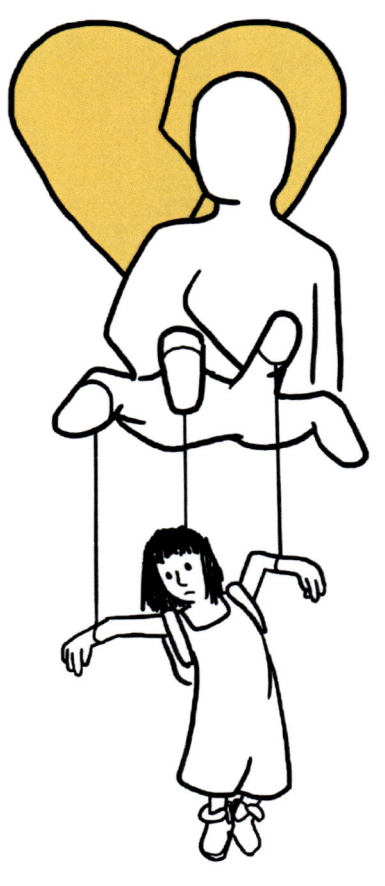

I'll apologise if you admit you messed up too.

I'm sorry

for whatever I did.

I'm sorry...

I was only giving constructive feedback.

That was the past.
Can we just move on?

Why are you trying to punish me?
Are you trying to make me feel bad?

I'm sorry but you do the same thing to me and I never bring it up.

I'm sorry. Why are you making such a big deal of it?

I'm sorry.
I was wrong
but if you
hadn't
pressured me
the way you
did, I would
never have
done it.

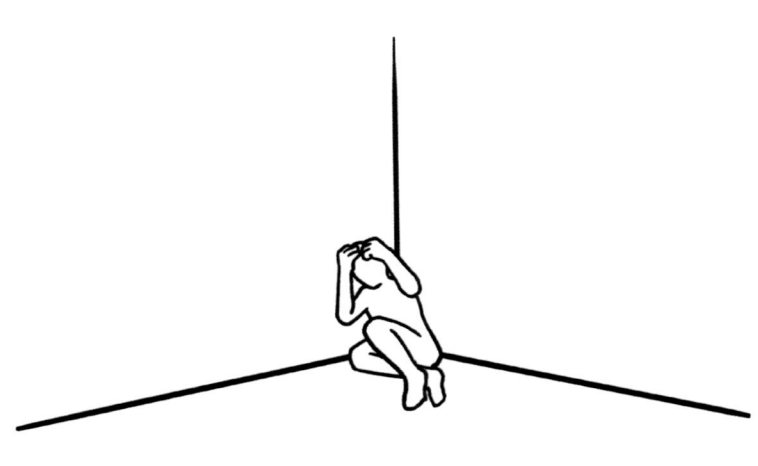

You have no idea how bad you made me feel about myself. What with your anger and blame...

I found myself looking for positive attention elsewhere.

If you were not so angry, it would be easier to apologise.

I'm sorry if there are things I've said that upset you.

I'm sorry

you feel that way,

but you need to understand my position

too.

I know I've said this before, but I'm sorry for doing it again.

I'm sorry

if you felt hurt
by what I said.

Mistakes were made...

I apologise if I did anything wrong.

I'm sorry but I was just being honest.

I regret this situation has occurred.

It's unfortunate things turned out this way.

Let's
just move
on and
start again.

If Mary Poppins was here, she would suggest:

"Acknowledge you know what it was you said that hurt and take responsibility for it."

I'm sorry.
I was wrong.
I care about how my words and actions affect you.
I want to be a safe place where you can be honest.
I want to listen to how it made you feel so we can fix it and reconnect.

I love you.

Epilogue

The scary part in truly apologising is admitting to being the villain – accepting having done something wrong or made a mistake and conceding to be being far from perfect.

Here are some practice tips. Share them with your loved one.

There are three essential elements to an apology:

1. Admit guilt. You were wrong or mistaken, and are, at least in part, responsible.
2. Promise to try to do your best and not to do it again. This is not who you want to be and want to do better.
3. Make an honest and open effort to fix the relationship. Appreciate the worth of the other person and show that you care.

There is no guarantee an apology will fix things. One can hope but never expect forgiveness. Apologies are not a trifling, passing thing. Done badly (or not at all) can end a relationship. Done well, they might consolidate it.

Acknowledgements

Once again, many thanks to the wonderful Jane Ormond and Luke Harris – who make up my team in putting my books together. My work would still be on my desktop in desperate need of an edit and formatting if it were not for you both.

And a huge thank you to Thomas Corboy who has excelled in capturing the nuances of Lil' Kaz. You are a delight to work with and your illustrations bring the pages to life.

And of course, thanks to Dom, Stef & Louis. *Sorry, not sorry...*

www.ingramcontent.com/pod-product-compliance
Lightning Source LLC
Chambersburg PA
CBRC101309020426
42333CB00011B/84